VINCENT'S PRAYER

VINCENT'S PRAYER

VINCENT JAMES CONNORS

Copyright © 2017 Vincent James Connors

The moral right of the author has been asserted.

Apart from any fair dealing for the purposes of research or private study, or criticism or review, as permitted under the Copyright, Designs and Patents Act 1988, this publication may only be reproduced, stored or transmitted, in any form or by any means, with the prior permission in writing of the publishers, or in the case of reprographic reproduction in accordance with the terms of licences issued by the Copyright Licensing Agency. Enquiries concerning reproduction outside those terms should be sent to the publishers.

Matador
9 Priory Business Park,
Wistow Road, Kibworth Beauchamp,
Leicestershire. LE8 0RX
Tel: 0116 279 2299
Email: books@troubador.co.uk
Web: www.troubador.co.uk/matador
Twitter: @matadorbooks

ISBN 978 1788037 310

British Library Cataloguing in Publication Data.
A catalogue record for this book is available from the British Library.

Typeset in 11pt Garamond by Troubador Publishing Ltd, Leicester, UK

Matador is an imprint of Troubador Publishing Ltd

To my lovely wife Christine and daughters Mandy and Christina for all their love and support throughout the years, not forgetting my four beautiful grandchildren, Charlotte, Matthew, Matilda and Lucie.

VINCENT'S PRAYER

Light up my morning, O Lord of the sunshine,
Transcend my lonely life to happier times.
Carry my burden, for you are the stronger
Lift me from darkness to light so divine

Be you beside me, O Lord, ever watchful
Look out ahead for the pitfalls that wait
Lead me O, shepherd, lost lamb in the desert
Home to the saving belief in your grace

Teach me, O Teacher, you of all knowledge
The wisdom to know the things that are right
Life ever lasting, for those who believe in
The awesome persuasion in your gentle might!

Wrap your cloak round me, O Lord my defender,
Block out the fears that persist in my head
Grant me that peace, that seems to elude me
I who am troubled… and living in dread!

Hold my hand firmly, O Lord of the traveller,
Walk you beside me, and I know I will cope

Show me the path that leads to your Kingdom
Path of the peaceful, path of all hope

Clear this confusion, O Lord of all logic,
Sort out my life in your order of things
Banish the darkness, you, light in the tunnel
Fly with me homeward… on gossamer wings.

WE MANIC INSANE

Down in the depths of a
Mist shrouded forest,
There's a deep swirling water
By a tree covered lane,
And it's calling your sons
It's calling your daughters,
To come and to dance
On it's ghostly white waters;
It's calling the broken
It's calling the lame
It's calling the manic insane.

It's two in the morning
And down in the forest,
There's a man in confusion
Just, walking around,
Yet I heard it said
That he once resided
In the largest, oldest
House in the town;
But now, the asylum's closed down.

Now he's going for a walk
To the dark swirling water,
For it's calling your sons
It's calling your daughters,
It's calling the people
Who jump from steeples,
It's calling the bleeding
The people in pain;
It's calling the manic insane.

There by the edge of that
Eerie dark water, stands a
Young man in terror
Eyes, staring and cold,
But, don't go too near him
You might feel his sorrow,
Oh, don't look in his eyes
You might see his soul;

And if you don't want to
You don't have to listen
To the desperate cries of
A soul who's in pain…crying
'Eli! Eli! Lamasabachtani
Don't forsake us…
We manic insane!'

I'M CALLING ON YOU, LORD

I'm calling on you, Lord,
I'm calling on you,
To save you calling on me.
I know that you're busy, Lord,
Sometimes quite dizzy
Righting the wrongs that you see.
But, I'm feeling lonely, Lord,
All on my only,
Need someone to talk to you see,
So I'm calling on you, Lord,
I'm calling on you
To save you calling on me.

They're felling the woods, Lord
And that can't be good –
To make matches to burn what is left.
The chainsaws devour, hour upon hour,
Yet they tell us they know what is best.
But you made the woods, Lord,

For years they have stood, Lord,
All blooming in glory to Thee,
So, I'm calling on you, Lord,
I'm calling on you
To save you calling on me.

They've poisoned the rivers, Lord,
It gives me the shivers,
When I think what they give us to drink;
Oh! It couldn't be whiskey, Lord,
It's something more risky
A concoction of effluent stink!
With the seas filled with oil,
Just give them a while
They'll walk on its surface like Thee,
So, I'm calling on you, Lord,
I'm calling on you
To save you calling on me.

They're clogging the highways, Lord,
Yes, and the byways
With 'Dagenham Dustbins' galore!
And they say they've no room,
Lord, they'll build to the moon
And I'll bet they'll come back for more–
They're wrecking your beauty, Lord,
I feel it my duty
To report the destruction I see,
So, I'm calling on you, Lord,

I'm calling on you
To save you calling on me.

They're killing the whales, Lord,
From boats without sails
In the interest of science, they say,
This slaughter and plunder
Has reduced their number,
To the point of extinction today.
Lord, make them willing
To cease this crazed killing,
To swim your great oceans so free!
Oh! I'm calling on you, Lord,
I'm calling on you
To save you calling on me.

They've a junk-yard in space, Lord,
Not far from your place,
With satellites whizzing around!
They've cameras on Mars,
Photographing the stars
Flashing images back to the ground.
Yet, right here on Earth, Lord,
The place of your birth
There are people who hunger and need!
So, I'm calling on you, Lord,
I'm calling on you
To save you calling on me.

'Tomahawk Cruise Missiles'
Make an eerie type whistle
As they fly like bats out of Hell!
They can find their own way
By night or by day
With a plastic microchip cell.
How the people will cry,
As they look to the sky:
"Lord, does the bell toll for me?"
So, I'm calling on you, Lord,
I'm calling on you
To save you calling on me.

LIVING TOMBS

They take art from the people
And lock it away,
In pantheons grand, museums of today.
Then they hang slum graffiti
On pristine gallery walls,
And place ancient statues
In marble aisled halls
And they call to the 'Pilgrims'
With faces of doom,
To come and pay homage,
In these living tombs.

So they come and pay homage
And speak in hushed tones,
As they tip-toe in reverence
Through these graveyards of bones.
Their aesthetic views don't matter a lot,
For they are told what is beauty
And they're told what is not.
And the child whose graffiti
Once lit subways of gloom;
Is reduced to a genius,
In these living tombs.

As they move through this 'Road Church'
Sacred objects they roar:
'Yours not to reason but gape and adore!'
King Tut' and his treasures lie
In time-warped-deep freeze;
Yet, this 'Boy King' has left us
But, proof of his greed.
As they move through the temple
To the dead march, in tune;
These ranks of dead people
In these living tombs!

SONNETS

Now all those days of loving are long past,
I number you amongst the golden corn,
Those days of loving were not meant to last,   (1)
And bitterness can quickly turn to scorn.
It's not enough to say that I was wrong,
For right, or wrong, it matters not a fig!
It only mattered when our love was strong,
And then, all spent, we had no more to give.
Sometimes, at night, I gaze upon the moon,
And in its face I see your furrowed brow,
And know now that we parted all too soon
But sadly, that was then, and this is now.
Yet in your lonely eyes I see your pain,
And hear your cry: 'Our love was all in vain!'

My blighted rose, what stories can you tell?   (2)
O! You that once was lovely, now are scorned,
But was your beauty in your perfumed smell?
Your power in the treason of your thorn?
When all your seasons came and went with ease,
Then all the world admired your changing dress,
But now that you are blighted and diseased,
Then, surely, you must know they love you less.

But I, for one, remember you in bloom,
You danced to breezes for the summer sun,
And bowed your head in reverence to the moon,
Admired by all who passed by, every one.
But, beauty's only enemy is time,
Its legacy will be a bitter wine!

HAWTHORN TO ASH

Children are dreamers, and so are the aged
But a child dreams in colour, the old dream in rage
Oh, I was a dreamer when I was a boy
When I lived in a land of magic and joy
Where the sun would come up, or go down in a flash!
Where I ran through the trees
From Hawthorn to Ash!

Down by the Black Water I met the Banshee
Entranced by her beauty, when she beckoned to me
"Come now, movourneen, run this comb through my hair"
As I did so, I swear I heard symphonies fair
But one look in her eyes and in terror I dashed!
And I ran through the trees
From hawthorn to ash!

The fairies were wailing and wringing their hands
At a funeral, led by a leprechaun band,
Slow marched through ferns where they disappeared
Drums muffled in black, so the dead wouldn't hear
How I scurried for home, when the lightening did flash
And I ran through the trees
From hawthorn to ash!

Now that I'm older, I too dream in a rage
For life's lost its colour, it's a black and white page
Yet, my thoughts often stray to when I was a boy
When I lived in that land of magic and joy
Where the sun and the moon would collide in a crash!
Where I ran through the trees
From hawthorn to ash!

THE TRIBES

The bomb that killed the baby
Was planted in a drain,
The I.R.A claimed it was they
Behind this act of shame.
How dare you bastards claim
This deed was done in Ireland's name!

I too am of that country
And you don't speak for me,
For who would take an infant's life
Just to make a nation free?
Ah, 'The Last of Europe's Stone-Age-Men'
Would do it, easily.

Such acts will not rekindle
That patriotic fire
For, that flame's long been pissed on
By the peasant and the squire,
A stinking pile of ashes
Upon a funeral pyre.

'For God and King and Ulster!'
Were those the words you said

When in God's name you took O' Kane
And shot him through the head?
Another Fenian bites the dust,
Just one more Papist dead!

I too am of that country
How dare you speak for me!
For who would kill a man
Because he's of a different creed?
Ah, 'The Men of Sixteen-Ninety'
Would do so easily.

You preach from Holy Scripture
Yet drag it through the mire,
But, that book's long been pissed on
By the bigot and the liar;
A desecrated 'Holy Book'
Upon a funeral pyre.

BLACK JACK

Black Jack lived beneath the stairs,
A small dark cupboard was his room
And for company, he had three friends,
A mop, a bucket and a broom.

The children, with respect and fear
Crept quietly past Black Jack's door,
Afraid that Black Jack just might hear
And rage at them with mighty roars.

They really felt there was no hope
He kept them all awake at night,
Getting drunk on liquid soap
And causing arguments and fights.

He ordered Mop to mop his brow
He ordered Brush to brush his hat,
And screamed at Bucket, 'Water now!'
While lying on a sheepskin mat.

He felt superior to his friends
To Mop and Bucket and to Broom,
Slowly driving them round the bend
In that dark and dingy little room.

Then came a lad from Tír-na-nÓg,
To confront Black Jack with his sins,
He spoke in a gentle Irish brogue,
His name was Fergal 'Mighty' Quinn.

Now Fergal was a plucky boy
The bravest lad in Tír-na-Nóg,
Though not much bigger than a toy
He would defeat this Black Jack rogue.

BLACK JACK

The children's eyes were wide with fear
As Fergal opened Black Jack's door,
He was using Bucket for his beer
While Mop and Broom cleaned the floor.

Then there was a deathly hush
As Fergal stood on Black Jack's hat,
Black Jack made a drunken rush
But fell back dazed upon the mat.

'I am Fergal Mighty Quinn
From the magic land of Ti-na-Nóg,
And I confront you with your sins,'
He said, in a gentle Irish brogue.

'You and I have met I'm sure,'
said Fergal Quinn to angry Jack

'You were a stinking toilet brush
Before you went all bald and daft.
Then someone 'green' recycled you
Nine leather tongs into your head
Renamed you Jack of Nine Tails
Instead of Dirty Smelly Fred.

'They let you live beneath the stairs
With Mop and Bucket and with Broom
You bullied them and made them scared
In that dark and dingy little room.

'You really thought that you were tough
Forgetting what you were before
A dirty stinking toilet brush
Sitting on a toilet floor.

BLACK JACK

'But I am Fergal 'Mighty' Quinn
From the magic land of Tir-na-Nog
And I give back your hair again
I make you what you were before.

'Jack! I banish you back to the loo
To the lowly place from whence you came
To gorge yourself on toilet brew
And never scare a child again!'

CAROL FOR THE HOMELESS

I had a sense of déjà vu
As the weary party came in view,
The weather was a freezing brew
That grey December morning.

He led a donkey that was lame,
His pregnant woman rode in pain,
Through wind and snow and driving rain
That grey December morning.

His name was Jo, the donkey's Mo
And his lovely wife was Mary-O'
Searching for a place to go,
As Christmas was a-dawning.

In a run-down shack by a mucky track
Not far from a place called Letterfrack,
There, amid the oat meal sacks
Mary's newborn child lay bawling.

And Mary's heart with pride did swell
To see her baby look so well,
'I name this child Emmanuel,'
Born this Christmas morning.

Joseph said a silent prayer
For his wife and baby fair,
'Is this the child who will declare
A new-age-Christmas dawning?'

'The Three Wise Men' who came to see
Were Murphy, Madden and McGee,
Three pillars of society
Bearing gifts of hate and warnings.

'Get out! Get out! You gypsy louts
For we don't want your kind about,'
And church bells, they were ringing out,
As they left on Christmas morning.

THE ROAD TO BENEDICTION

The road to benediction
Was a free and easy road,
I had a child's conviction
My heart it bore no load,
For I believed that blessings
Would last till I grew old,
And take me down the road of life
To my eternal goal.

The road to benediction
was a bright and breezy way,
There were no contradictions
When I knelt down to pray,
For I believed that someone
Could hear every word I'd say,
A listener on the road of life
Till I was old and grey.

Now the road to benediction
Is an uphill rocky road,
Winds of time against me
Blew the incense from my clothes,
And all those childhood blessings
That had sanctified my soul,
I've wasted on the road of life,
I'm black as British coal.

Oh, the road to benediction
Is now winding grinding pain,
Once where there was sunshine
Is now lashed by driving rain,
And if I had one penny
For the names I've took in vain,
I'd be the Devil's millionaire;
Unholy and insane.

YOU AND ME

(A POEM FOR MY WIFE ON
VALENTINE'S DAY '93)

I loved you when I saw you
In that little Wiltshire town.
Your hair was black as ebony,
Your eyes were smiling, brown.
I loved you all that summer,
I loved you through the fall,
To me, you seemed so vulnerable;
Did I seem strong and tall?

But I think I loved you most
On the day that we were wed,
Not many words were spoken then
Yet, those few words we said
Have seen us through the sunshine
And seen us through the snow;
I loved you, truly, on that day
On Bradford's Manor Row.

The kids have grown, years have flown
So fast, to God knows where!
Yet still, we are together
We're one we are a pair.
Perhaps I loved you early
Perhaps I loved you late,
Oh, I loved you in the loving years
But more so, through the hate!

FINDING THE WORDS

You've that look in your eyes,
James Clarence Mangan,
It tells me you've something to say
And God knows I've waited
To hear those words stated,
Why not ask me today?
How many years now
Have we been a-courtin'
It must be ten years or more,
Don't you think it's time
You asked me to marry?
For my heart is aching and sore.
We've been together now
Since the blackberry picking
All those years ago after the fair,
But I'll hold on forever
If that's what's required,
That's how much that I care.
Oh, I know you're a man
To whom words don't come easy
But you know what my answer will be,

For I love you so much,
James Clarence Mangan,
I'd swim any ocean for thee.
Oh, My Dark Rosaleen,
Your beauty beguiles me
I can't find the words to be said
And just when I think
I know how to phrase them,
They fly right out of my head.
Yes, it's true what they say
If we go on a-courtin'
We'll not be married but dead,
So I'll try to ask you
The best way I know that
Words of love should be said.
Can you see yonder gravestone
It casts a long shadow –
All carved in a Celtic design?
Well, how would you fancy
A gravestone just like it
With your name carved next to mine?
Oh, it is a strange way
To ask you to marry,
But I did it the best way I could,
For I love you so much
I don't want to tarry;
My lovely Rosaleen Dubh.

CATHEDRALS

The first cathedral that I knew
It wasn't built, it simply grew –
Right from the ground up to the sky
With trees that reached to the on-high
And I would swear I heard them say
Thank you, Lord, for this lovely day.

There were no priests or bishops there
In marble pulpits to declare
That we would all be sent to hell
Because we couldn't stand the smell
Of incense… and pomposity!

How we ran the woods so free
Madigan, McGrath and me
And as the sun went down each day
We fell upon our knees to pray
And in that stillness we would say
Thank you, Lord, for this lovely day.

We felt a nearness to creation
Madigan, McGrath and me
A sense of humble adoration
As the sun shone through the trees
And the birds sang in the choir
Thank you, Lord, for days like these.

Now I've returned to my cathedral
I've seen the others, York and Paul's
Felt no solace or redemption
Felt no presence there at all!

Still, the trees reach to the heavens
Crying out in anguished pain
Jesus! Can't you see we're dying?
Please, Lord, stop the acid rain!

FACES ON MY BEDROOM CEILING

Faces on my bedroom ceiling
Sometimes blooming sometimes wan
Mind is spinning wild and reeling
To a time when I was young

Pock-marked portraits in the plaster
Gives the young an acne look
Makes the old the butt of laughter
Warty noses bent and hooked

Scenes out of the Sistine Chapel
Hazy, now they disappear
Children, laughter, pears and apples
Somewhere down my childhood years

Concentrate the mind on staring
Strange the scenes the mind creates
Mother Theresa face of caring
Adolf Hitler face of hate
Drowsiness affects my vision
Pain will wipe my canvas clean
Just an object or derision
All spaced out on drugs and dreams

Bedroom clock that speaks in flashes
Modern, silent, awesome truth
Every flash one second passes
Watch the passing of my youth!

THE POWER

Oh, a fearful thing this power,
People calling by the hour just to say,
Thank you for the light of day, and for
The fright your presence commands.
They have no qualms about their
Insignificance in its awesome presence.

The sound of feet on city streets
Reverently entering through mansion doors
Roofs adorned with towers and spires
Ever upwards reaching higher
To touch the power above.
Earthly fools with heavenly rules
Too blind to see the power is free-

Not sitting in some gilded tomb
Where body stench would make you
Swoon, and singing hymns and praying
Calls that never reach beyond the walls
I doubt if they're heard at all.

Hear the Wizard with his blizzard of words
Dressed to shock, not sanctify; he'll never get
To heaven, not wearing that kit,
What a pompous twit! And the grunter
Bible thumper preaching fire and brimstone
On well burnt ears. He speaks so well with
Tales of hell, I swear you could almost smell it!

When I went to see the Power, I walked on carpets
Of wild flowers, and threw my arms around
The Pillars Temple, just to feel the sway.
No flash of light or roar of might announced
Its holy presence, just a whisper in the trees
Barely audible in my ears said:
'The power is here!'

THE WARRIOR

Just a simple pile of stones was all
That bore witness to his passing
There on the wild Alberta prairie;
Blackfoot Indian warrior once fierce
And quick, now at peace and still,
To the lee of Watching Hill.

Did the shaman priest intone him
To his final rest? Was he of
'The Ghost Dance Council'
Who's rhythmic dance of fear,
Prayed for the buffalo herds return
The white man hoards to disappear?

The shinook wind was blowing
As the prairie night came in,
And I settled down to rest the night
To the lee of Watching Hill,
When I saw wild Indian ponies
Run before a lightning storm;
Oh, it made my heart grow warm.

But what was it that brought me
To this wild and lonely place?
This habitat of prairie dog
And deadly rattlesnake,
But the lonely seek the lonely place
And each go hand in hand;
Like him, beneath the prairie stones
I'm just a lonely man.

Yet I have seen huge monuments
Proclaim men's bloody deeds,
Great monuments to vanity and greed
But unlike him beneath the prairie stones;
They are not of the warrior breed!

SOMETHING MISSING

(MEMORIES FROM CHILDHOOD)

Two by two, they would shuffle up the lane
Towards the convent on the hill
Arms folded inside the wide triangular
Sleeves of their black religious habits
Heads bowed, they moved like Chinese
Mandarins shuffling in the evening sun
Rosaries and crucifixes dangled with the
Children from broad black leather belts
And I, a child, believed the whole wide world
Was ruled by Irish Catholic Nuns.

We children cried our love to the
Face of the 'Mother Don'
But no reaction ever came our way
They just shuffled, on and on to paradise
To the convent on the hill, to where
Stout walls shut out such childish things
Where they, the chosen, would remain
Till morn, minds transcending to a higher plane

Where dirty children are already grown
And canonized as saints.
And every morning back they came
These six mute saints upon the lane
They never felt the children's pain
Or heard their cries of love
Now bolstered by their renewed guarantee
Of eternal life.

The day I left to go to school in the
Valley of Sliabh na mBan, the Matron
Combed my scruffy hair, and there was
Expectation in the air when she said
That I would love it in Clonmel
For there, she said, the smell would be
Of mountains and of mountain heather
And then Miss Drennan sat me on her knee
And cupped my tiny freckled face in
Her huge loving hands, and looking deep
Into my frightened eyes she said:
'You know that I will always love you.'

IT WAS THEN THAT I KNEW
WHAT WAS MISSING!

The Valley of Sliabh na mBan = The Valley of
The Mountain of The Women.

ANGELA

(For Malcolm's Daughter on her 40th, 8th Oct. '98)

Angela Merrick, forty years,
Big brown eyes filled with tears,
Oh, I never had a fear;
That you would grow up lovely.

Little girl, you brought me joy,
More than any little boy,
With a look, Oh, all so coy;
'T' would melt my heart completely.

In my old mind I see a trace,
Of a pretty baby's face,
Happiness all dressed in lace;
Going to a party.

And you sang a children's song,
Sang it all that summer long,
Now those summer days are gone;
And I'm approaching winter!

HAWORTH MOOR

Hear the wind howling and growling and scowling
Roaring its fury across wild Haworth Moor,
See the soft heather head bowed to the weather
Like a carpet being fouled on as the deluge unfolds
From skies that make faces on high haunted places
Where Cathy and Heathcliff retreat from the cold
In the finest love story that ever was told.

See the moon shining on eerie Top Withens
Casting strange shadows across wild Haworth Moor
The night sky is speckled with bright astral freckles
Of stars whose light dance is a joy to behold
In skies that make faces on high haunted places
Where Cathy and Heathcliff in the heather will stroll
In the finest love story that ever was told.

See the sun shining on eerie Top Withens
Spreading its warmth across wild Haworth Moor
The blue-speckled heather head raised to the weather
Greeting the sun as a rare friend but true
From skies that make faces on high haunted places
Where Cathy and Heathcliff will never grow old
In the finest love story that ever was told.

SIMON PETER

(Late of Cartwright Hall)

He walked the streets of Bradford Town
In a staggering, drunken sway,
Wore boots that let the seasons in
And a coat of shabby grey,
His address was quite exclusive
That's had you wished to call;
For he lived in his stench
On a council bench,
By stately Cartwright Hall.

They called him Simon Peter
That's because he was a rock!
And he chose his lair
With the utmost care
By the Lister Floral Clock,
It didn't go tick! It didn't go tock!
And it never chimed the hours;
But, Simon knew the seasons
By the beauty of the flowers.

'The Sally Ann' do the best they can
But insist on sobriety,
And for Simon Peter (sometimes eater)
It was the crux of the matter, you see,
For that hostel bell like the road to hell
Demanding sober hours;
So, he chose his bench in his bin-bag stench;
Watched the dying of the flowers.

When the cock crowed loud for Simon
In Lister Park so fair,
He was much too drunk to hear it
And soon too dead to care,
But his pain, at last, was over,
All seasons finally run;
There beside his floral clock
At the rising of the sun.

LITTLE CHILD

Little child sleeping in my arms, I love you;
Jesus, now you're here the world is saved!
Holy child, with stars so bright above you;
I, your mother, Mary am afraid!

Long before you were my Christmas baby,
The Angel Gabriel, spoke to me within:
Told me that your life would not be easy;
Said you'd come to rid the world of sin.

Saw the days of glory in your teaching,
When you cured the lame and raised the dead;
Why then, little Christ Child, am I weeping:
Rocking in my arms your sleepy head?

In my dreams I saw you ride to Zion,
Triumphant, on a donkey shaggy brown:
People waving palms call you Messiah!
Others, jeering, said you were a clown!

When you stood afraid, betrayed and lonely
In the garden, called Getsemene;
Oh! My keening wasn't for you only;
Jesus mild! It was for you and me.

Christmas Child I need to hug you nearer;
I can see the pain on down the years.
Little Jesus. How I love you dearer;
Seems to me it all will end in tears!

Hush! Now, little Jesus, while I ponder,
How you'll drag that Cross to Calvary,
I, your mother Mary, pray in wonder;
Knowing my Little Child will set us free!

A HAIKU A DAY

He entered by night,
And leaving as he entered,
Left only his shame.

The rain storm cried tears,
That ran down the nigh time glass,
And then it was gone.

Autumn leaves falling,
A technicolor dream coat
For cold winter days.

Naked winter trees
Embarrassed by the weather
Freezing in the storm.

Ghostly garden swing
Blowing gently in the breeze
The children long gone.

The nights drawing in
But the light in the window
Will mark my way home.

The new creation
The season of hope returned
Glad tidings to spring.

LIMERICKS

There was an old tramp called McGee
Who claimed he was smarter than me
He booked into a hostel
Where the bugs were quite hostile
And fled when attacked by flea.

There was a young fellow called Lens
Who lived in the Lincolnshire Fens
His accent was rare
But he didn't care
For culture is rare in the fens.

There was an old lady from Surry
Whose fields were laden with slurry
The slurry was stinking
But she got to thinking
How slurry might make a good curry.

There was an old man from Clonmel
Whose feet had a terrible smell
He went to the stream
Himself for to preen
And the fish cried out, 'Bloody Hell!'

There was an old nun who was praying
But didn't know what she was saying
She asked for a beer
To bring her good cheer
And now, out cold she is laying.

I once met a lady from France
And asked if she wanted to dance
We danced through the night
Until the dawns light
And now she won't give me a glance.

I saw a man stand in a river
He suddenly started to shiver
The current was strong
And swept him along
The last time he'll stand and dither.

UNDERSTANDING

Reject all your hatred
You'll feel so much lighter
Take on more love
You'll feel much more free
Look to the sunshine
And life becomes brighter
We're all on life's highway
Together, you see.

Cast your face skyward
When the rain is pouring
Roar at the thunder
In a louder reply
Ride on the storm clouds
In a wild world of wonder
Pick your own star
To put by.

Walk in the forest
And see the wild flowers
Stop and behold them
And you'll feel no strife
See their perfection
You're drawn to their power

One moment well spent
In your life.

Look through the eyes
Of a child who is smiling
You'll see no hatred
In eyes such as these
Through the eyes of a child
The world's more beguiling
More children and laughter
We need.

Reach out and touch
The face of your brother
Race, creed and colour
Will all disappear
We are all one
We're all one another
Reject all suspicion
And fear.

So, call me a fool

I'll call you my brother
Call me your friend
I know I'll agree
Look to the rainbow
Choose your own colour
Let's slide down to earth

THE SENTINEL

You could guarantee that he would be there,
Leaning over the half door,
Features as gnarled as his shillelagh,
With clothes that grew on him like parasitic moss,
A ragged old sentry observing what passed for life
On Barrack Street.

His beard was wild, un-pruned, like a blackthorn bush
That might have housed a bird's nest,
But what bird would sing in such a face
Without being choked to death!

Pollution of that forest was constant –
From the clay dudeen clasped between
His dirty rotten teeth, black and yellow,
Like an old neglected out of tune piano.

Rory, his mongrel dog, would run round and round
In circles, barking his excitement
Tethered by a chain to the earthen floor,
Man and dog, like creatures from an ancient bog
Would greet me at the door.

Oh! I was afraid of Tom Feracum,
For his topic was always on death!
And often I would hear him say:
"Did anybody hear a trumpet play?"
Old Tom was waiting for the Judgement Day!

"AGH! You'll know the day of judgement
When it comes," he would say from behind
A smoke screen, penetrated by a throaty spit!
"For after Gabriel's trumpet, you'll see
A great white line across the heavens, a
Sort of bothareen to the Creator,
'Tis then you'll know for sure."

And when I saw my first jet vapour stream,
I thought it was the day; I'll bet old Tom could
Hear my frightened screams –
It's here! It's here! It's
It's the Judgement Day!

Oh I was afraid of Tom Feracome!

OPPORTUNITY LOST

Was I so blind that I could not have seen
the love displayed within your lovely eyes?
Now, too late, I know just what it means.

Wasted days just flowed away like streams
that rushed towards the sea to meet the tide,
Was I so blind that I could not have seen?

Lonely, when I think what might have been,
had I but known my place was by your side,
Now too late, I know just what it means.

You had beauty, more than Egypt's Queen,
walked with confidence and regal pride,
Was I so blind, that I could not have seen?

Words of love that poets rhyme and ream
in volumes, are but fantasies and lies!
Now too, late I know, just what it means.

I will spend remaining days in dreams
wishing that with you I could abide,
Mocking wind that roars a haunting keen,
Now, too late, I know just what it means.

A PINDER FIELDS PRAYER

It was his smile that caught my attention through my drug-induced haze. Fixed at an angle, like a careless lipstick imprint he had forgotten to erase. His sunken eyes were staring… staring quite uncaring, as if his mind was out to play. And questions met with no response at all. Not of movement, or of sound. Living statue, set in time; since the day the fate of stroke had gunned him down!

So, why all these tears running down my face? Salty taste dampening my pillow. Weeping willow, crying just because my legs refuse to work? Self pitying burke! I who once could dance, yet never gave a glance to life's limbness charioteers. I who felt uneasy when the cripple came too near. Now cripple! learn to cope! and look in hope at 'Staring John' across the ward and cry aloud: 'Thank you, Lord!' Oh, bless this 'Staring John', Lord, and hold him in thy care.
This my humble plea, Lord, my lonely Pinderfields Prayer.
Amen!

SEVENTY-FIVE KIDS ON A STATION WALL

We could hear the steam trains puffing
From Lismore to Cappoquin,
The excitement when the whistle blew
Soon it would be in,
The wild scramble for positions
From the shortest to the tall;
There was seventy-five kids
On the station wall.

We must have looked peculiar
To the people on the train,
Seventy-five coconuts
On a fairground stall arranged,
But even more peculiar
Seen from our side of the wall,
Was the patchwork quilt of colours
On our backsides all!

The patches on our backsides
Would put 'Joseph's Coat' to shame,
A wall of technicolour dreamers
Wishing we could drive the train,
But the one who came the closest
To the dream was Micky Finn;
Backside patch, gone in the scramble
Let the train smoke in.

They said that Micky's dad
Would visit sometime in the Spring,
So, with wide-eyed expectation
He watched the trains come puffing in,
He would recognise him easily
He'd be handsome, dark and tall,
Spring changed her gown to autumn;
Micky still watched from the wall.

The day we saw the future
I find east to recall,
A sound like 'Gabriel's Trumpet
Sent us rushing to the wall,
Oh, the sight, it mesmerised us
As we watched the train roll in;
The first time that a diesel train
Had entered Cappoquin.

Oh, I know the trains no longer run
From Lismore to Cappoquin,
And that my old school, St. Michael's
Is now 'Guesthouse Mrs Flynn's'
But should that goodly lady
Hear a lonesome whistle call;
She'll see seventy-five ghosts
On the station wall.

IF I COULD CHOOSE

If I could choose a song to sing
A song of freedom it would be,
Proclaim aloud, my freedom hymn
That all mankind be free.

The face of love that I would choose
Would be my own sweet mother's face,
Never knew the love I'd lose –
Long gone, without a trace.

For happiness I'd choose three days
The first would be my wedding morn',
The others go without a say;
The days my girls were born.

If I could choose one powerful word
To shine upon the way we live,
I do believe with all my might;
I'd choose the word, forgive!

If I could choose a time of peace
A time before the pain and hurt,
Before life started or deceased;
That time before my birth!

MO PA! MO PA! DO YOU REMEMBER ME?

As I stand here staring at the simple metal cross that marks your final resting place,
I know, for certain, two things: You did exist. And you are not immortal.
For immortal, is what you seemed to me, through the eyes of a child.
Can you see or hear me, from this, your last long bed? I hope so.
For there are things that I must say, things you may not want to be reminded of.

Do you remember how you beat me and little Michael Welch, for bringing shame on the school.
You sent me to fetch 'Black Jack' the cat o' nine tails from beneath the stairs.
And our crime that day? You caught us five year olds eating a slice of bread and butter,
Coated with sugar, given to us by Michael's widowed mother.
There was no mercy or forgiveness in response to our cries that day,

As the nine leather thongs ripped into us.
So, what did that, and other numerous cruelties down the years teach me?

Now that I'm a man, I know that forgiveness is surely more powerful than hate.
That tears are only liquid pain. And that adversity can be turned to advantage.
You see, Mother Patrick, I wrote the pain of 'Black Jack' right out of my head,
In a poem for children. And now I don't cry anymore… not really!
But more than all this I want to say: I Forgive You!

Ah yes! Before I leave you to the lonely emptiness of eternity to your last, long bed,
That, which you spent your whole life dying for, there's one more thing I must say.
The humble cross above your head proclaims to the whole wide world that:
Your surname is Russell. How strange, how very very strange, that a bride of Christ
Should have such a very ordinary name!

Russell, Indeed!

THE GYPSY BAND

Clop! Clop! Horses hoofs resound
As the gypsy band rode into town,
Piebald ponies, white and brown
And caravans so grand;
Here comes the gypsy band!

Sat up front at the caravan door
Was a handsome rogue, Freddy Ward,
To Jane Mulhearn he was a lord
He'd come to ask her hand
Here comes the gypsy band!

And the people cried:
'Stand to your post!
Nail down the things you value most!
Pray to the Father and Holy Ghost!
Here comes the gypsy band.'

That night Freddy met with Jane,
She talked about the family shame
How to father she'd explain,
Her love for this wild man;
From that gypsy clan.

And a voice it said:
Where lovers tread
Don't let them part you, Jane and Fred
For that is 'no man's land',
Don't ask for father's hand.

Hush! Hush! Horses muffled feet,
At dead of night Jane took her seat
On the duckboard of his caravan neat,
Now they've children sweet and grand;
Here comes the gypsy band.

ABOUT THE AUTHOR

Vincent James Connors is a native of County Waterford and has lived in the UK for more than fifty years. Unfortunately, ill health forced him to leave the civil service, but this forced retirement lead to Vincent taking up writing as a hobby, and he has since had a number of short stories and poems published.

Many of the author's poems and stories have been inspried by his life events and childhood, and the author is married with two daughters, and four grandchildren.